Rainbows & Straitjackets

By Jessica Jackson

"Find what you love and let it kill you."
    - Charles Bukowski

"My whole life is a dark room. One big dark room."
    - Marilyn Manson

"The blazing fire makes flame and brightness out of everything that is thrown into it."
    - Marcus Aurelius

Those guys know what's up.

BEAUTIFUL RUIN.

I want you to **crash** into me…

But Fuck, it's gonna be a **trainwreck**.

In the soft light of dawn
You make all of my mistakes look like

A beautiful love song

With a tragic ending.

Stay with me a while longer.

Let me remember.

This will all end soon.

The smoke from your cigarette curls around us - a ghost with nothing left to haunt.

"Why are you here?"

I hear the confession beneath your question:
this is the invitation to admit what neither of us is allowed to say.

I love…

The smell of cigars.
The clink of poker chips on the table.

And the adrenaline of making bad decisions.

Have no regrets:

For there was a time, a place and a virtue.

And it was exactly what you wanted to do in that time and place…

Virtuous or not.

I want to remember you verbatim.

Every lie.

Every stinging truth.

Every almost.

I'm at a crossroads:
One path is dangerously exciting.
The other is dangerously safe.

Don't open the curtain; don't let the light in.

Then it will be daytime and we'll have to stop dreaming.

You're the constant thrill, the electricity of a thousand first dates.

He is the warmth, the calm and the safety of forever after.

And I am the fool wedged between desire and safety...

Always choosing the burn.

I'm going to tell you to stop soon.

I need you not to listen to me.

Whisper to me.
The promises we made,
The lies we swore were plans,
The fantasies we dressed as futures.

I'll swallow every word.
We both know none of it is true.

This will never be over.

Just whisper.

You're my dirty hotel room.

I'm your 3am.

You're my cheap wine.

I'm your cigarettes.

You're my black stilettos.

I'm your lipsticked shirt.

You're my kiss goodbye.

I'm your favourite game.

You're my Arsenic.

I'm your Heroin.

We're black cats.

We're secrets.

We're toxic.

Kiss my neck again, I want to feel the warmth of you as it traces over my skin from the inside.

I want to forget that secrets are bad.

I want to pretend…

Pretend this isn't a mistake, that we're the only two people who ever learned how to touch.

Pretend we aren't a curse.

Pretend this isn't borrowed time.

Keep your eyes closed….

I want to pretend.

"*I'm mesmerised by you,*" he says.

Breathing the words into her skin, as if confession were a gentle thing.

Everything shifts.
Everything deepens.
Everything damns us.

Everything has changed now.

Don't worry, I'll sing the words for both of us.

Then it's my fault if they're wrong.

I gave you the knife.

I told you to twist it; twist it until it bleeds.

Only when I felt the blood dripping from my spine
did I know that I was living.

I didn't realise until too late that I'd taught you how to kill
the parts of me that still felt alive.

So many unspoken words between us…
And I don't know which ones I'm allowed to say.

You're my addiction and my muse.

You're all the things I need and all the things I shouldn't have, bound together in one torturous entity.

I can't quit you.

You are excruciatingly exquisite.

I could spend days tracing the lines of your skin.

Now that I've touched you,

now that I've tasted you…

This can never be over.

If only I could find a way to rewind our story…

we'd **burn** beautifully,
break loudly,
and **forget** softly.

It's just you and me in the dark.
The curtains are drawn, the world can't get us here.

Make me believe.

Make me forget.

"Don't fall in love with me," he said.
But gravity has never listened to warnings.

I didn't stand a chance.

You, me, Florence.

So, what do we do now?

Just go with it.

…. Just go with this.

The juxtaposition of your heart and mine...

What a beautifully delicate and fucked up notion.

It's still pitch black outside and I'm on your door.
It's been raining all night and my clothes are soaked through.

It doesn't matter if you don't let me in;

I just need you to know I love you before the sun
comes up.

But maybe...

Letting go will be like flying...

A kind of freedom I've never survived before.

And when the sun sets....

The shadows become all of the darkness that
you deserve.

When I hear
your voice on
the line, All I
can think of...

Is how I want to watch you bite your

Bottom Lip.

I want to
feel the
warmth of
your breath
on my neck,

while your hands
tangle in my hair.
I want to watch
your eyes get
darker.

As I become the only thing you know
right now.

Let me love you right now,
Dance with me.

Kiss me like you taste forever on my lips,
Even if it's only in the moment.

Dance with me.
Just this time.

Every day
I notice more and more
That you're not the person, that I decided you were.

And I want you more now *(against my better judgement)*
Than I ever did –

Back when I
thought you were
less
Than everything you are.

I want to feel your elbow
In the small of my back
As I arch my spine
Against you.

Wrap your hand through my hair
And slide it down to my throat.

Tighten your grip.

More.

Tighten it.

So I can finally breathe.

If you asked me to tell you what I was thinking...

I'd lie.

Because the truth isn't poetic –
It's the way I want to run my hands down the wreckage of
your past.
Trace the scars you don't talk about.
Feel the weight of everything you've carried,
like I'm trying to learn the blueprint of a collapsing building.

I'd be lying, if I didn't say

That you feel like the person that will finally help me sleep.

But I'm not about to hand you that kind of power over me.

So instead, I'll lie.

And tell you
That I'm thinking of the controversial state of North Korea.

I keep my eyes closed
When you kiss me

So I can't see
The goodbye in your eyes.

Light up a cigarette between your cherry lips...
I want to take you for a ride.

Don't worry about who's watching. They're only jealous that you're mine.
Spread those long legs of yours, baby. Come sit with me...
I've got a secret.

Spike your stilettoed heels into the ground, feel me underneath you
Know that you're turning me on.
Drink your whiskey straight, enjoy the burn as it slides to the back of your throat.
Let it remind you that pain is the only things that never lies.

Open yourself to me, let me see all of you.

I like that they can see too; they all want to feel the lines of
         your skin.
Look me in the eyes, so I can tell you what I want you to do.
I know you want me to.

Bite your bottom lip, make it bleed.
I want to see it drip from your mouth as I pull your hair.

Arch your back.
Feel for it.
I want you to push back on my hand as I touch you.

I want to watch you give yourself over to me, as I control your
         breath.
We're just two more casualties in a world that stopped
         counting.

I'll take you to the edge, I'm not sure if I'll let you go over yet.

Convince me.
Show me that I should let you.
Maybe I'll say yes.

Light up a cigarette between your cherry lips...
I want to take you for a ride.

People watch us like we're dangerous.
Funny thing is –
We're not even trying.

We're just surviving badly.

Hotel bathroom.

Again.

I want you. But it's not love. You know that.

You've got that edge that I need right now. You're my gateway drug. Nobody gets me high like you do.

Turn me on, it's alright. Leave the door open.

You turn your back and that's okay with me. I don't need to see your face right now.
You're my cheap thrill. Everything about you turns me on.

I like the silhouette of you on your knees in the cheap hotel room.
I like the way you taste.
I like watching you put your dress back on before you leave.
I always block the door one last time.

There's something about you I can't let go.

I want you. But it's not love. You know that.

I'm still here; shut your eyes.

Will you leave me?

No.

Why?

Because I need you now. You're under my skin.

You said we were too different.
That it wouldn't work.
That's not true.
I would've given up air for you.

I love you to the point of madness.

I never told you; you're my high.

I hate how close you stand to the edge.
I want you to come back.

If you jump –
I'll understand.

But God, I hope you don't.

I'm waiting for you to save me.
I'm counting on it.

I use my quiet moments
To think of you.
And all the beautiful things we
Told each other,
Without speaking a word.

If there are words for you, then I don't have them.

… And here's to all the sleepless nights.

And somewhere down the line,

Between sleepless nights and waxing lyrical on every curiosity
We could devour from each other…
We became philosophers and
Began to quote ourselves as though our intricacies

Were some sort of gypsy gospel.
Fuelled by days of deviant sex and
Fantasy fires,
We thought nothing of stepping on landmines
And speculating from the wayside.

There is no greater fuckery than the human mind…
And honey, yours drives me wild.

I remember when we met; we were so young back then.
The kind of young that breeds immortality and chaos.

We told each other everything we thought we knew...
Which, as it turns out – was nothing.

I remember tracing the lines of your young skin,
Not really knowing much about what lay beneath.
Not that it mattered – I couldn't have fixed your pain back then.
I remember thinking you were beautiful.

You're not the man that I met all those years ago,
Amidst the immortality and chaos.

Well, parts of you are.
Now you have silver in your hair, scars on your hands,
And tales of past lovers on your body.

But your eyes are still fire and your heart is still wild.

Somehow,
Time has made you more beautiful.

Tell me you'll never leave.

I'll never leave.

Are you lying?

I don't know.

I want you to kiss me

In the same way, every day
Until the world forgets our names.

Rendezvous... What a delicious word.

It's too late, I love you now.

I'm falling for you.

I know it's going to hurt when I hit the ground...

But I don't care.

Promise me you won't stop when I tell you to.

I can hear your soul.

Your hands speak louder than your voice—
piano notes drifting like confession.

You trap me with a sense of freedom that I can't get
anywhere else.

I want to be your favourite mistake.

But you…

You're the kind of heroin a man ruins his life for.

GHOST NOTES.

I still have that locket you gave me.
We were so young back then.

It's all tarnished, the pictures have faded, and it doesn't close properly anymore.

But I still have it.

It's my favourite locket in the whole world.

Everyone has their own reasons for burying the past.
Mine?

Simple.

I long for it too much. It's destroying me.

You'll always be that perfect love that I had but couldn't keep.

I wish I could have my first kiss again.

The awkwardness, the excitement, the electricity...
I'd give anything to feel that kind of magic.

You said I never listened;
That I forget everything.

And yet you never noticed that I remember you
verbatim.

We used to spend all our time
Laughing
And pretending we knew what
Was going on.

We used to sit around
And see who could tell
The biggest lies,
And make ourselves believe them
Even more.

We used to argue a lot
With common sense
Just to hear ourselves win,
Like being right meant anything.

We used to daydream
The rest of our lives up,
Creating anything and everything
Back when we thought the world
was ours to ruin.

We used to be young.

We used to know everything.

I won't be your last love.
But I want to be your greatest.

His lips always linger on her cheek a little longer than they should.

Close enough to cross a line,
Far enough to pretend he didn't.

Nobody ever notices.

They share a secret smile that doesn't belong to anyone else.

He stand a little closer than he needs to, just to breathe her in.

No one hears it except her –
that low hum of a song they shouldn't remember.

She hums it back.
Of course she does.

And nobody will ever know;
His lips always linger.

One day you'll fade from symphony to static…

You'll become white noise in the back of my mind.
And I'll mistake the silence
for healing.

And so it begins;

Heartbreak begins quietly –
then carves its initials
into every rib.

What weapon, I ask you – is sharper than a memory?

In that moment,
We lived like lovers…

In that moment,
We were perfect.

In that moment by the ocean,
we were infinite –

weightless and wild,
writing promises in the sand
that never survived the tide.

If I tell you
That I love you
Please just kiss me back.

Because it's only in this moment,

Where tomorrow never comes.

All the pretty girls
That fell for his smile
And let him talk them out of themselves –
In the same way, that same slow motion suicide
Every time.

His words are all nothings
That cleverly create a façade
Of everything.

He built moments that looked beautiful
If you didn't stare too long –
Hollow scenes.
Cheap magic.

Stage lights over an empty room.

He doesn't remember them all.
Too many faces.
Too many nights.
All the same.

His restless hands and silent fingers
Fold paper flowers and
Search for new skin
When the silence gets sharp.

And all the pretty girls
Smile and wave
At the ghost of a man they never met.

I wonder if it's easier to be you.
It's getting too hard to be me.
Nearly impossible.

She was so perfectly broken.

In that quiet, deliberate way.
The kind that made her beautiful –
Not despite the cracks,
But because of them.

She collected moments, she said;
Flashes of heat and light
Like lightning in a bottle.

She let the memories fade
Before they could cut her open.

She spent her whole life
Close to the surface
Protecting her diamond heart
From hands that didn't deserve it.

He picked up her broken
And she sank into his skin
Fighting to remain unchanged.
He held her as she lost her mind and finally
Became real.

Don't say what this is – Don't give it a name.

Because that makes it real.

Then we'll both know what we know.

And then this has to be over.

I thought we had matching scars.
But yours was just a scratch.
And mine never healed.

She lives in sepia,
reviving the past
because the present
never feels loud enough.

If I'm gone when you wake up, don't go looking for me.

My story has been written and you're there on every page.

Don't ask questions you know will remain unanswered;

Just remember all the pages that we wrote together in the sunlight of our life.

Breathe in softly…

And let the light touch your face as you whisper goodbye.

He cried while she stared forward.

Out of words.
Out of endings.
Already gone.

I wrote this sober, but it tastes like whiskey anyway.

There's nothing altruistic about the way our souls met.

Love is just a ritual soaked in gasoline.

The world hums like a cheap amp, buzzing under our sins.

We lit our own fires
And made our own Gods.
We worshipped nothing but survival.

Smoke-stained hours,
cheap whiskey truths.

Still digging through the ashtray
for something worth keeping,
even if it's just proof
that we made it through another night.

Everyone's carving themselves up these days.
Filtering the parts of themselves that are human.

New noses, new lips, new faces…
Like the old ones committed some unforgivable crime.

They queue for perfection
under fluorescent lighting,
handing their fear to a surgeon
with a God complex and a payment plan.

They trade their faces like used cars –
scrapping the dents, repainting the exterior,
pretending the engine isn't still coughing smoke.

They come back swollen, bruised,
smiling through the ache like martyrs –
as if pain is proof they're finally worth looking at.

It's so strange watching the world
try to fix itself, one incision at a time.

Is the answer:

    a) The spaces between the teeth on a comb
    b) Western post–war architecture
    c) Loneliness.

I fill my days with **thoughts** and memories of you. Otherwise they'd be empty.

We said vows on the rooftop,
where the city blur turns people into ghosts
and ghosts into witnesses.
Exactly where misfits belong.

No guest list, no spectacle…
Just a handful of faces to confirm it was real –
These two maniacs gambling with their forever.

It didn't feel like a wedding.

It felt like setting fire to the version of ourselves
that never believed we'd make it this far.

It was beautiful.
It was metal.
It was a whirlwind.
It was intrinsically ours.

FAULT LINES.

I like living in the city.
It feels safer,

packed tight inside a paradox -
never-ending white noise
so loud
you can't even hear it.

My favourite part
is the white-collar subversion of small,
mindless acts.
Fleeting glimpses of the most futile anarchy -
so small
most people miss it.

The cigarette butt beneath the recycling sign.
Junk mail scattered
with almost religious intent.
The woman who crosses before the green man appears...
And the steering-wheel bandit
who baptises her with his rage
as he tears past.

I live to watch
these upper-class zealots of order
unleash the mildest fury imaginable,
safely wrapped
in their own capitalism.

The only person being real
is the burnt-out addict pacing the street,
screaming at the wind
without restraint.

But she's only doing it – being real -
because she's high as FUCK.

And that's the start of yet another Red Wine Story.

Same poison, different night.

Some call me a heretic.
I never fit the script –
I was born sideways,
thinking too loud,
breaking every quiet rule
the world tried to hand me.

I never learned how to worship
anything that kept me small.

Quietly wandering
Down the street,
She stops to pick up
A silver coin.
A small smile plays on her lips
As she turns it over
In her palm.
Because
She always looks for the glitter
In the tarnish.

As she keeps walking
An old man with gnarled fingers
Stretches out his bony hand.

She drops the silver coin
in his hand.

And he smiles
His crooked smile.

The soles of her shoes
Are so worn from
Walking
That her feet drag
On the hot bitumen.

Everybody looks upon her
With disinterested pity;
Nobody saw
She had diamonds
On the inside.

Take it off.

All of it.

I want to see the real you.

I thought I was nothing…

You taught me I was everything.

Place your struggle in my hands.
I promise I'll try to take away the pain.

There is a house near my street
with a sign in the window that reads:
Promised no trees cut down.
Liar. Pants on fire.

Painted in block letters,
each sentence spat with disdain –

a cryptic taunt
left out to dry.

I like to imagine the author
as a tightly wound centrifuge,
existing for one purpose only:
to discharge anger
in half–haikus
for passing strangers.

No one knows which tree was cut down.
No one knows whose pants are burning.
But everyone knows that sign.

It's written on a large
white flag –
either an oversight,
an epistemic failure,
or the quiet logic of a soul
defeated by a broken promise.

A surrender disguised as protest.

Hopelessness expressed
in the most apathetic form
he could manage.

I want to kiss you in Paris.

I don't like you because you're perfect.
I love you because you're imperfect.
Perfectly so.

How do you do it?

Do what?

Be you – do what you do.

Well if I'm not this person and do what I do, somebody else
will inevitably become a version of this person and do some
modicum of what I do.

I might as well wear the straitjacket with my name on it,
instead of someone elses'.

Nietzsche once said,

"All truly great thoughts are conceived by walking."

Which tracks,
given our transport systems are swollen
with excessive users –
heads down, thumbs twitching,
scrolling for permission
on what to think next.

If Nietzsche was right,
then mastery begins with movement:
owning your direction,

captaining your own trajectory.

This is where good things are born.
This is living free.

So the irony isn't lost on me –
self-driving cars entering the world
at the exact moment
we're offered payment plans
for weight-loss injections,
to chemically erase the bodies
we no longer move.

My son is my muse.
He inspires me to breathe.

I always sit in the middle row of the bus.

Even though mine is the last stop,
I've never felt the
Self-assured confidence
That you need, to sit in the back row.

I also have my life together
Just enough
To not need the safety bars of the front row.

So I sit here, in the middle,
In the atrium, equidistant to the
Extremes of inner-city commuting…

Japanese piano music rushes from my earphones
Filling my ears and welcoming me back
To the concrete jungle.

Do you have enough money to save your soul?

Don't try
And simplify me.

I'm so much more complex
Than that.

Do you promise?

I promise. Hang in there.

We wear our
Stories on our skin –

Battlefields masquerading as art.

We paint away our lives
With restless fingers
For all the world to see.

And we're okay with that.

What soothes the savage beast, right?

My darling…
We're a storm, you and I.

Eyes of fire,
Lightning hearts,
Thunderous souls
And electric bones.

Say you'll remember me.
Tell me you'll haunt me.
Promise me you'll always be my muse...
Even when the ink runs dry.

In the deafening roar and blinding lights of a concert that neither of us knew anything about...
You taught me about who you were.

You grew up on an island and you like coriander
(I hate coriander).

You're also a Pisces.

I told you about how I like to write and dance and daydream about saving the world.

You have a tattoo of a marlin
And I have a tattoo of a ladybeetle.

We only knew about 4 songs that the band played.
I still don't know if our star signs matched...

I don't think they did.

In the blinding noise of a crowded bar,
we learned who we were:

Two **strangers** pretending
we weren't already colliding.

Religion is architecture.
Belief is instinct.

Fortitude Valley comes alive at night –
in that half-feral shift cities make
when the sun finally stops judging them.

The young and hopeful
spill onto the streets…
dropping pills like communion wafers,
swallowing cheap vodka
like it might wash the week out of their bones.

The whole valley comes alive –
sweat, neon, chaos,
and those ridiculous, beautiful moments
where two drunk idiots cling to each other
like they've finally cracked the code to existence.

They haven't.
But it's sweet watching them believe they have.

They dance too hard,
feel too much,
fall apart in alleyways
and laugh maniacally a minute later (just before the second
drop).

Neon chaos wrapped around human wreckage –
a whole suburb of beautiful trainwrecks
trying to outrun who they are
until the lights come back on.

We spend all our days

Making all of these paper planes....

And we don't even know if they can fly.

Everybody has a little crazy, right?

My cat stalks me around my house,
like he's disappointed in my entire personality.
Bold opinion from someone
who's never survived more than ten minutes outdoors.

He growls at birds
with all the swagger of a drunk in a barfight –
loud, dramatic,
and scared shitless.

I swear he looks at me
the way people look at fires –
half curious, half convinced
I'll burn myself eventually.

It's cute because he's a cat.
If he were a person,
I'd have blocked him years ago.

I wonder if forever is longer than tomorrow.

You can paint a brick,
film a cat walking across the road,
tape a banana to a wall…
Call it art,

and someone out there will swear it saved them.

That's the trick:
nothing becomes meaningful

until a person decides it is.

Art doesn't have to be perfect.

It just has to hit someone in the ribs.

Simple – and that's kind of beautiful in itself.

I'm an artist.

It doesn't pay the bills,
but it's so fucking fun to throw around colours
like a toddler methed up on sugar…
And write nonsensical didactics that
Punch people right in the soul -
Just because I gave meaning
To an otherwise meaningless cacophony
Of visual ADHD.

Somebody asked me the other day how much I love my spawn.

I said, "That's easy. He is the sun. He lights up my whole world, and without him I would perish."

ACKNOWLEDGE MENTS.

This book was written as an open letter to acknowledge all those I love, those I *have* loved, those that love me... And those that used to love me. Maybe even to those that will love me, someday.

There's also some rambling about self-love and loving all the world has to offer, in the most paradoxical way possible.

So I guess in hindsight... this was another of those million books about love. But I say fuck sometimes in it, which adds a twist of lime.

We have all both created victims and been the unknowing victim, caught in the collateral damage of life's complexities. But there are so many beautiful moments, both in the tarnish *and* the vibrancy of the world - we find our equilibrium somewhere in between.

Thank you to all the beautiful people that have lent me a part of their lives in order to create this book (often unknowingly).
I hope that I represented the vignette of your moments in a way that feels true and real to you.

To my husband Jax: thank you for your endless patience with me, and for celebrating my boundless energy with me every day. And sorry about my boundless energy.

To Perks: thank you for letting me into your story, and I love that it has a happy ending.

To my son Jett: you always have been - and always will be - my greatest muse. I love you more than everything.

J. xx

ABOUT
THE
AUTHOR.

Jess lives in Brisbane, Australia with her husband, son, and 2 cats.

She is an artist, velociraptor enthusiast, avid disliker of capsicum, and entirely unapologetic about her excessive energy, optimism and relentless plans to save the world.

Jess started a charitable project called Mera.Ki in 2010, as a way to give back to the community.

Proceeds from all associated artwork sales (including this book) go towards supporting the homeless community and raising awareness for mental health challenges.

For more information, go to:

www.merakiartstudio.com.au

ARTISTS SUPPORTING

CHANGE.

A catalogue record for this book is available via the National Library of
Australia at www.catalogue.nla.gov.au
Book design and layout by Mera.Ki Collective.
ISBN 978-1-764636-0-7

www.ingramcontent.com/pod-product-compliance
Lightning Source LLC
Chambersburg PA
CBHW022004090426
42741CB00007B/890